GREAT PETS

Small Dogs

Joyce Hart

mc Marshall Cavendish
Benchmark
New York

Marshall Cavendish Benchmark
99 White Plains Road
Tarrytown, New York 10591-5502
www.marshallcavendish.us

Library of Congress Cataloging-in-Publication Data

Hart, Joyce, date
Small dogs / Joyce Hart.
p. cm. — (Great pets)
Summary: "Describes the characteristics and behavior of small dogs,
also discussing their physical appearance and place in history."
—provided by publisher.
Includes bibliographical references and index.
ISBN 978-0-7614-2995-1
1. Dogs—Juvenile literature. I. Title.
SF426.5H375 2008
2007036784

Front cover: A Welsh Corgi
Title page: A Basenji
Back cover: A Cavalier King Charles Spaniel

Photo research by Candlepants, Inc.
Front cover: Mark Raycroft / Minden Pictures

The photographs in this book are used by permission and through the courtesy of:
Shutterstock: 1, 9, 24, 20, 35, 38, 40, 44, back cover. *Corbis:* Bohemian Nomad Picturemakers, 4;
Peter M. Fisher, 8; Charles Gold, 13; Yann Arthus-Bertrand, 16; Robert Dowling, 27;
Ariel Skelley, 39, 42. *The Image Works:* Mary Evans Picture Library, 6. *The Bridgeman Art Library:*
Half-Seated Dog, Mexico, Proto-Classic, 100 BC-AD 300 (Earthenware), Colima Culture /
Museum Of Fine Arts, Houston, Texas, USA, Funds Provided By Meredith J. Long, 7. *Alamy Images:*
Van Hilversum, 10; Patrick Brown, 29; Thorsten Eckert, 36; Tbkmedia.De, 43. *Super Stock:*
Age Fotostock, 12, 14; Marilyn Conway, 31; Piper Lehman, 32; Jerry Shulman, 37.
Elynn Cohen: 18. *Brian Buerkle:* 25. *Peter Arnold Inc.:* Bios Klein & Hubert, 21; S.Muller, 26;
Phone Labat J.M. / Rouquette F., 34, 41. *Minden Pictures:* Mark Raycroft, 19, 22 ;
Mitsuaki Iwago, 28. *Photo Researchers Inc.:* Alan & Sandy Carey, 23.

Editor: Karen Ang
Publisher: Michelle Bisson
Art Director: Anahid Hamparian
Series Designer: Elynn Cohen

Printed in Malaysia
6 5 4 3 2 1

Contents

1

Little Friends

Historians believe that as far back as 15,000 years ago, people kept dogs to help make their lives a little easier. Illustrations of dogs have been discovered in ancient cave paintings. **Fossils**, or ancient bones, of small dogs have been found near human bones. These are clues that tell us ancient peoples included small dogs in their daily lives.

In some cultures, small dogs played important roles in religion and society. For example, small **breeds** like the Pekingese and shih tzu were very important to the Chinese thousands of years ago. The shih tzu and the Pekingese dogs were sometimes called lion dogs because the long hair around their heads looked like a lion's mane. The Chinese believed lion dogs guarded against evil spirits. Only members of royalty, such as **emperors** and their families, were allowed to keep these dogs. The small dogs probably also protected the royal families by barking when danger was near. Some

A lion dog sculpture stands in front of a building in China. Many believed that lion dogs protected their owners from harm.

Many small dogs, such as this Cavalier King Charles Spaniel, were treated like little furry family members.

historians think that these small breeds were often kept inside the big sleeves of the robes worn by emperors or empresses. The dogs helped warm their owners and probably were used to attack anyone who tried to hurt their owners.

Small dogs lived in many palaces and castles all over the world. French kings and Italian queens loved having little dogs they could keep on their laps or nearby. These animals were often very spoiled. Some had their own servants and rode in small carts made just for them!

THE CHIHUAHUA

With its big eyes, big ears, and very small body, the Chihuahua is an easily recognizable small-dog breed. However, many people do not realize that this breed has been around for more than a thousand years. The Toltecs and Aztecs, the ancient people of Mexico, believed that the Chihuahua was a special messenger from the gods. Paintings of Chihuahuas can be found on the walls of pyramids in Mexico.

Chihuahuas are the only dogs that are native to Mexico and Central America. Christopher Columbus wrote about Chihuahuas in his diaries. Columbus may have been the first person to take Chihuahuas back to Europe, where they quickly became very popular pets.

This sculpture of a small dog—possibly a Chihuahua—was made more than two thousand years ago by the people who lived in the region that now includes Mexico.

Not all small dogs lived in palaces. Different breeds of small dogs lived with ordinary people. These small dogs worked hard on farms and in homes. Many were also treated as treasured family members.

Big Jobs for Small Dogs

Though most herding dogs are medium or large breeds, many ranchers use small dogs to herd their sheep and goats.

Small dogs have many natural **characteristics** that have always made them good workers. Some small dogs even helped their owners prepare meals. For example, people trained small dogs to turn mills that ground grains to make flour. The flour was used to make bread and other foods. They also trained dogs to turn a spit, a long pole that hung above an open fire. Food hung from it, and the dogs turned the spit so the food would not burn while it was cooking.

Many small-dog breeds are great for working outdoors. Pomeranians, were first raised to herd sheep. Some terriers were used to keep mice and rats away from homes and businesses.

In the past and today, many small dogs help their owners hunt. Beagles, a small type of hound, love to hunt. Hunters often use beagles to help track down small animals like rabbits and foxes. Although dachshunds have very short legs, they are great hunters of badgers and foxes. Their short legs allowed them to crawl into underground badger and fox holes. Spaniels are also good hunting dogs—they love to run through woods and swim in water. They help find ducks and other wild birds that their owners hunt.

Small dogs also have very important jobs that help people every day. Many are trained to use their keen sense of smell to locate dangerous things in public places. For example, you may have seen a beagle or some other small dog sniffing luggage at an airport.

Small dogs are also used to help people who are disabled or ill. With special training, the dogs guide their owners through streets and other places, help them handle certain tasks at home, or warn them when danger is near. Many owners and their small dogs visit hospitals or nursing homes to cheer up the people staying there. With so many wonderful qualities, it is no wonder that small dogs are some of the most popular pets in the United States.

Hearing dogs, such as this Chihuahua, are specially trained to help people who are deaf or have problems with their hearing.

9

2

Is a Small Dog Right for You?

It takes time and energy to care for a dog. They depend on their humans to make sure they are safe and healthy. Bringing a dog into your home is a big responsibility.

Do You Have Time to Care for a Small Dog?

As with all pets, you must be willing to spend time caring for your small dog. Your pet needs to be fed, groomed, trained, and exercised. All of these things take time and patience.

Spending time with your dog is very important. You need to bring your dog out to go to the bathroom and to exercise. Dogs that do not get enough

Some families enjoy having more than one small dog in their home. These two beagle puppies were adopted together.

exercise often become sick and develop health and behavior problems. Also, most dogs do not like to be left alone for too long. If they are left out in the yard by themselves for too many hours, some dogs dig holes under fences

and run away or get hurt. If dogs are left inside the house by themselves for too long, they might destroy things, bark for hours, or go to the bathroom indoors.

Training is an important part of owning a dog. Your small dog needs to be **housebroken**, or taught to go to the bathroom outside. With training, your dog will learn to obey commands and behave properly. However, it takes a lot of time to train a small dog. You must be willing to spend this time for training. Little or no training can lead to your dog getting hurt.

Certain breeds of small dogs have special needs. For example, long-haired breeds need to be brushed every day because their fur can get tangled. Small dogs with very little hair or fur need special care for their skin.

Chinese crested dogs require a lot of grooming and special care for their sensitive skin. Before choosing a small dog you should learn about what kind of care different breeds need.

Do You Have Space for a Small Dog?

Unlike big dogs, small dogs do not need a lot of space. This is one reason why many people who live in apartments keep small dogs as pets. It is important to remember, however, that small dogs still do need some space. A small dog needs a place for its bed or its **crate**, its food and water bowls, and its toys. Your small dog will also need room indoors to walk around

Before bringing home any new pet, think about whether or not other pets in your home will accept the new addition to the family.

and play. Most small dogs have small feet and delicate toes that can break easily if they are accidentally stepped on or squashed. You must be sure that there is enough space in your home for you and your family, your small dog, and any other pets you already have.

Be sure you have somewhere to walk your dog outside. Besides needing to go to the bathroom outdoors, your dog should be allowed to get some fresh air and sunshine every day. A fun walk down a quiet sidewalk or a romp in a dog park are perfect ways for you to spend time with your little friend. Before you get a small dog, make sure there are places nearby where you can do these things.

Puppy or Adult Dog?

There are good reasons for choosing either a puppy or an adult dog. It is important that you think about which one would be best for your home. Before you make up your mind, think about the differences between bringing home a puppy or an adult dog.

Puppies are cute and small and cuddly, which makes them seem like the best choice. They are full of energy, too, so they are fun to play with. If you bring home a puppy, you will have a lot of fun watching it grow up alongside you.

When they are teething, puppies like this terrier mix need special chew toys or treats. Without the proper chew toys, a teething puppy may destroy furniture, clothes, shoes, and just about anything it can put into its mouth.

However, puppies can also be a lot of work. If you choose a puppy, remember that most puppies usually have had little or no training. You will need to spend a lot of time housebreaking it and teaching it how to behave inside and outdoors. Also, puppies lose their baby teeth just like children do. As a puppy's adult teeth grow in, the puppy will chew on just about anything it comes across. This can be a problem if you have very small children in your home or if your family is worried about the puppy destroying furniture or other household items. Special chew toys made for puppies can help when puppies are teething, but most puppy owners have lost a few shoes and some furniture to those sharp little teeth.

Puppies also become lonely very easily. They are used to spending a lot of time with other dogs. As a result, when the puppy is left alone for the day or at night to sleep, it may cry a lot or go to the bathroom indoors until it is used to being alone.

Often, an older dog will be calmer than a puppy if it has been trained and properly cared for. So an adult dog may not need quite as much training as a puppy. Many older dogs are already housebroken. An older dog might also come with a list of good **traits**, or behaviors. For example, someone at the place where you get your older dog might be able to tell you if the dog is gentle with children, knows not to bite, and comes when you call its name.

Whether you get a puppy or an adult, having a small dog to share your life with can be a wonderful experience.

3

Choosing Your Small Dog

Once you are sure you are ready for a small dog, you need to make some more decisions. You should have an idea of what kind of small dog you would like. Then you must find a good place from which to adopt or buy your dog.

What Small Breed Is Best for You?

There are many different breeds of small dogs. Dogs that belong to a specific breed will have similar characteristics. For example, all cocker spaniels have long, floppy ears, while Chihuahuas have big ears that usually stand up. A **purebred dog** is one with parents or grandparents that belong to the same

Pekingese have long fur that requires a lot of grooming. Some Pekingese owners bring their dogs to groomers who keep the dogs' fur short.

This mixed-breed puppy is called a doxle because it has beagle and dachshund traits.

breed. A **mixed-breed dog** has parents that are different breeds. A mixed-breed dog might have some traits of both breeds. For example, a cocker spaniel and beagle mix might have the body of a beagle with the curly coat of a cocker spaniel. Besides physical features, breed characteristics can also include energy levels, natural skills, or personality types. For example, some breeds are high-energy dogs that need to run around a lot. Some breeds are better swimmers, and some breeds can be very stubborn or hard to train.

Before you pick out a dog, do some research. Find out what traits each breed has. Some breeds require more care than others, so you should learn all you can before you make your decision. You can also attend local dog shows to learn about different breeds. At a dog show you can see how different breeds look. Also, most of the people who show their dogs can answer questions you might have about the different breeds.

According to the American Kennel Club (AKC), there are more than one hundred pure breeds of dogs in the United States. The American Kennel Club places these dogs into eight separate groups. These groups are based on the breeds' traits. Small-dog breeds usually fit into five of these groups.

The Sporting Group

The sporting group includes dog breeds—small and large—that have natural outdoor skills like hunting or swimming. There are two different small breeds in the sporting group—the cocker spaniel and the Sussex spaniel. These small spaniels naturally have a lot of energy and love to run. They

The cocker spaniel is a popular breed of small dog. Its size and gentle manners often make it a good family pet.

also love to dive into water. This is why they were often used to help hunters. The smaller of these two breeds is the cocker spaniel. A full-grown cocker spaniel can weigh about twenty pounds and can measure around fifteen inches from the ground to its shoulder. Sussex spaniels are about the same size as cocker spaniels. Both the cocker and the Sussex spaniels are two of the best small dogs for families. In general, they are gentle, learn quickly, and are usually very good around children. Spaniels come in many different colors and have soft medium-length hair that can be slightly curly. Because they like to run, spaniels need daily outdoor exercise.

The Hound Group

Hounds are known for their tracking and hunting skills. These dogs use their strong sense of smell to locate things. Beagles and dachshunds are two popular breeds that belong in the hound group. Most adult beagles are about fourteen inches tall and weigh about twenty pounds. A beagle's fur is short and smooth. Most beagles have **coats**, or fur, that are a mixture of brown, white, and black. Beagles make great companions because they love to be

Some hounds, such as beagles, will howl a lot when they are excited or lonely.

with their owners. However, when they are left alone, they often bark or howl a lot. If you enjoy going on hikes and long walks, a beagle might be right for you.

The dachshund's German name means "badger hound," because dachshunds were bred to hunt badgers. Dachshunds are easily recognizable because they have long bodies and very short legs. Short-haired or smooth-haired dachshunds have a short coat that sits against the skin. Long-haired or wire-haired dachshunds have longer coats with fur that might be a little curly. Dachshunds are smart, but they can be stubborn and a little hard to train. They are very loving and devoted to their owners and do best in families with children older than seven. Because of

Dachshunds can come in a variety of coats and colors. The dog on the left is a long-haired version, while the one on the right has a wire-haired coat.

their hunting skills, dachshunds are also good diggers. So you have to keep an eye on them when they are out in your yard.

Basset hounds are another familiar breed. These small dogs have long bodies, short legs, and droopy features. Their ears are very long—sometimes nearly touching the ground when the dog is standing! A basset hound's eyes are also droopy, giving the dog a sad look. Many families love their basset hounds, claiming that they are loyal, affectionate, gentle, and sweet. Most basset hounds are short—only about fifteen inches tall—but they have a lot of heavy muscles and can weigh a lot. Some full-grown basset hounds can weigh more than fifty pounds! Be aware, though, like many hounds, bassets can howl a lot when they are lonely or when they want something.

Some dogs with long and droopy ears—like the basset hound—are more likely to develop ear infections. You should ask a breeder or a vet how to properly care for your dog's ears.

The Terriers

There are many different terrier breeds. Some are called ratters, which means they are good at catching rats and mice. Other terriers are good at herding farm animals. No matter which you choose, terriers often make good pets. One reason people like terriers is because they are very playful, very smart, and very curious. There are short-haired, long-haired, and curly-haired terriers, and they come in many different colors. Some terriers, such as the bull terrier, can be very stubborn and hard to train. Others, such as the fox terrier, are a little easier to train. Terriers have a lot of energy, so they need long walks and a lot of playtime with their owners. Some small terrier breeds include the cairn terrier, the miniature schnauzer, the Scottish terrier, and the Norwich terrier.

One of the most popular terriers is the West Highland white terrier. Called "Westies" for short, these white dogs grow to be about ten to eleven inches tall. Westies can make good family pets because they are alert, active, and friendly.

Westies are one of the most popular terrier breeds.

The Toy Group

This group is called "toy" because the dogs in this group are the tiniest of the small dogs. These dogs usually weigh ten pounds or less. Toy dogs have become even more popular because many people live in apartments and do not have much room for a bigger dog. Dogs in this group include the Chihuahua, Pekingese, shih tzu, Cavalier King Charles spaniel, Maltese, Pomeranian, and pug.

The second most popular breed in the United States belongs in the toy group. Yorkshire terriers are often called "Yorkies" for short. Yorkies have long, silky hair that needs daily brushing. Their cute looks and friendly personalities are just two of the reasons why they are a popular breed.

When its coat is not cut short, a Yorkshire terrier's fur can be so long that it touches the ground.

Italian greyhounds are tiny versions of regular greyhounds. An Italian greyhound usually grows to be about fourteen inches tall. A large greyhound can be almost thirty inches tall.

The toy group also includes small versions of large-breed dogs. For example, the Italian greyhound is a miniature version of a regular greyhound. Miniature pinschers are tinier versions of large Doberman pinschers. The toy group even has a miniature poodle. Over the years, miniature dogs were developed for people who liked the personality and looks of larger dogs, but wanted them to have smaller bodies.

A girl and her pet bichon spend some quiet time outdoors on a sunny day.

Non-Sporting Group

This group is made of dog breeds that do not fit into other groups. Popular small breeds in this group include the Lhasa apso, Boston terrier, French bulldog, Shiba Inu, and schipperke. The bichon frise is one of the most popular small non-sporting breeds. Its name is French and means "curly lap dog." Bichons are very smart and have easy-going personalities. At one time in the breed's history, the bichon frise was used in circus shows because it could be trained to do many tricks. Bichons have curly white hair that needs to be groomed frequently.

The Lhasa apso is another small breed that needs to be groomed often. Lhasa apsos have long, thick hair that comes in many colors. Lhasa apsos were first bred in Tibet, a mountainous country in Asia that can be very cold. That is why the Lhasa apso's hair is so thick. This breed of dog can be very friendly. The Lhasa apso was bred to be a watchdog, so you can expect it to bark a lot when someone new comes to your home.

The Lhasa apso gets its name from the Lhasa region in the Asian country of Tibet.

Where Can You Find a Small Dog?

There are many different places that sell dogs or offer them for adoption. However, not all of them are good options. The first thing you might want to do is to ask a **veterinarian**—an animal doctor—if he or she knows of any places that have small dogs for sale or for adoption.

A breeder usually specializes in a specific breed of dog. These puppies were raised by a family that only breeds bull terriers.

28

Shelters and humane societies have many different dogs in need of good homes. Some shelters have purebred dogs, but most of the adoptable dogs are mixed breeds.

The veterinarian, or vet for short, may be able to give you names of **breeders** who raise the type of dog breed that you are looking for. Most breeders specialize in one breed. A responsible breeder has been raising and working with that breed for several years. They breed their dogs to be judged at dog shows or to become treasured companions. Good breeders keep all their dogs healthy. All adults and puppies are brought to the vet for the necessary checkups and shots. Most breeders sell puppies, though many will also have older dogs for sale.

You can usually find a breeder through Web sites or ads in local newspapers or dog magazines.

Another good place to look for a small dog is at a local animal shelter or humane society. You can find the location of a nearby animal shelter online or in the phone book. Around the country, thousands of dogs are living in temporary shelters, hoping to find good homes. Some dogs might be in a

Pet Stores

Many pet stores sell puppies. However, most veterinarians and dog owners do not recommend buying a puppy from a pet store. Nearly all pet stores get their dogs from places that are more interested in making money than in breeding healthy dogs. Most of the puppies in pet stores are sick or are more likely to become sick— even if they look active, alert, and healthy. Before you buy a dog from a pet store, do some research. Find out if the puppy comes from a responsible breeder who raises healthy dogs.

shelter because their owners got sick and could not take care of their pets. Other dogs may have been abandoned or were found wandering loose outside. You can find both puppies and adult dogs at a dog shelter. Most shelters have mixed-breed and purebred dogs looking for new homes.

Whether you get your dog from a breeder or an animal shelter, you should always do your research beforehand. If you are looking into a breeder, find out how long the breeder has been raising the breed. Does the breeder have references, or names of other people who have bought puppies from him or her? If you are thinking about adopting a dog from a shelter, be sure to look into the shelter's history. Where do their dogs come from? How long has the shelter been open? Do the people who work at the shelter know a lot about dogs?

When you visit a breeder or shelter take note of the surroundings. Are the dogs kept in clean cages or kennels? Are there many small dogs crowded into small spaces? Do the dogs look active? Do any of the dogs look ill? If some of the dogs are ill, it is likely that others kept in the same place will also be sick.

When you are deciding on a particular dog, you should ask some of the following questions:

- How old is the dog?
- If the dog is in a shelter, why was it put there and how long has it been there?
- Has the dog been checked by a veterinarian?
- Is the dog up-to-date on all of its shots?
- How much exercise does the dog get each day?
- How does the dog react to children?
- How does the dog get along with the other dogs?
- Does the dog get along with other household pets, such as cats, guinea pigs, or birds?
- Is the dog housebroken?
- Is the dog leash-trained, and does it obey commands?

Many people think that small dogs are just the right size for cuddling.

Do not be afraid to ask these questions. Getting the answers will help you to bring home the small dog that is perfect for you.

4

Living with Your Small Dog

Be prepared for your new family member before you bring it home. All dogs need some basic things you can find at a pet store. Your small dog will need two bowls—one for water and one for food. The dog will also need a leash, a collar, and a name tag that hangs from the collar. The name tag will be helpful if your dog ever gets away from you. If your small dog has long or curly hair you will need to buy a brush. Your dog will also need a pillow or a small bed to sleep on. Some veterinarians recommend using a crate for small dogs. The crate gives your dog a safe place to sleep. It is also a good training tool used to keep an untrained dog from running loose or destroying things when it is left alone in the house.

This boy and his Jack Russell puppy are best friends.

A small dog needs nutritious dog food that is the right size for its small mouth.

Be sure to provide toys that are specially made for dogs. Human toys may break apart and make your dog sick. Your dog may like a soft toy to cuddle with or a hard toy to chew on. Pet stores have a wide variety of dog toys.

Bags and pet carriers are specially made for carrying your small dog. Always be sure that your dog has enough room inside the bag. The bag should also have openings or vents that allow your dog to breathe easily.

Vet Visits

To make sure your dog is healthy, schedule a visit to a veterinarian soon after you bring your dog home. Like humans, dogs need shots and medication to protect them from illness. The vet will examine your dog and let you know if it needs any special medication.

Vets often recommend putting a tiny microchip under your dog's skin. This identification chip has a lot of information about the dog and its owner. Unlike tags on a collar, the chip cannot fall off or get lost.

This pug is having its ears checked at the vet. Your dog's vet can help you learn how to keep your dog healthy and happy.

The vet can also tell you how much your dog needs to eat and what foods are best for your small breed. Ask the vet for tips on how to take care of your dog. He or she will be happy to explain how to housebreak it and how to care for its ears, teeth, and nails.

DOG DANGERS

There are many household items such as foods, chemicals, and plants that are dangerous to your dog. Eating any of these can make your dog very sick. If your dog eats any of the following, call your veterinarian or an animal hospital immediately:

- chocolate
- nuts
- coffee or tea
- onions
- human medication or vitamins
- mushrooms
- grapes and raisins
- mistletoe berries
- lilies
- aloe
- azaleas
- daffodils
- foxglove
- coins
- rubber bands
- string
- glue
- moth balls

- antifreeze (for cars)
- pesticides used to kill bugs or rodents
- cleaning products like soap or bleach

Puppies like this shih tzu do not know that string and other items can be dangerous. They will play with whatever they can find.

37

Besides bringing your dog in for regular appointments, the vet or nearby animal hospital should be used for emergencies. If your dog eats something it should not or looks like it is sick, do not hesitate to contact your vet's office. Careful attention and quick action can help save your dog's life.

Training Your Dog

Training your dog means that you teach it how to do many things. One of the most important things your dog needs to learn is how to go to the bathroom outdoors. If you live in a house, you can teach your dog to relieve itself in the backyard. If you live in an apartment, your dog will learn to relieve itself when you take it for a walk. Housebreaking is different for every dog. Some learn it very quickly, while others will take several weeks or months to be housebroken. With time and patience, however, almost every dog can be properly housebroken.

When training your dog, you might decide to attach its leash to a harness instead of a collar. A harness sits around the dog's chest and shoulders. This Boston terrier loves to go for walks when he is wearing his harness.

Most dog trainers and vets suggest rewarding your dog's good behavior with dog treats.

You should also teach your dog how to behave indoors and outdoors. He or she must learn to walk on a leash when outdoors. Walking on a leash protects both you and your dog. An unleashed dog can run away or be hurt by a car, a bicycle, or other animals. You might also get hurt chasing after your dog. Some cities and states have leash laws which require you to keep your dog on a leash at all times when you are outside. Your dog can also learn commands such as sit, down, come, stay, or go.

Some dog obedience schools have special agility classes that you and your dog can take. These classes teach the dog to follow commands to do fun activities, such as jumping over obstacles, weaving between poles, or climbing through tunnels.

Training a puppy is different from training an older dog. You can read books about dog training or you can find Web sites that will give you ideas on how to do this. The best way to train your little companion, however, is for both of you to attend some sort of dog obedience class. Many vets' offices and pet stores offer training sessions for puppies and for older dogs. There are even dog-training schools that specialize in classes for dogs and their owners. At these classes, teachers who have spent years working with dogs show you the proper way to train your dog. Obedience classes are also a good way for your dog to get used to being with other dogs. Proper **socialization** is important so that your dog learns to get along with other dogs and with other people.

Many small dogs can be trained to fetch a ball or a toy, roll over, or shake your hand.

When bathing your dog, be sure to use shampoo or soap that is specially made for dogs. Some shampoos and soaps that humans use can hurt your dog.

Time with Your Dog

Besides training, there are many other ways that you can give your new dog the attention it needs. One way is simply playing with it. Every dog is different, so your dog may not like the same games that your friend's dog likes. Some dogs love chasing a ball and bringing it back so you can throw

All dogs need some form of exercise. Chasing after a Frisbee can be fun for owners and their dogs.

it again, while others are not interested in playing fetch. Your dog may only want to run or jog next to you. Just remember, whenever you play outside, always make sure you have your dog on a leash, or be sure to stay in a securely fenced area.

Time spent indoors with your dog can also be fun. Brushing or combing your dog can be relaxing for both of you. Many dogs just want to be petted or cuddled. You can keep your small dog near you when you watch television, read a book, or do your homework. Many people like to read to their

Though they may be little—like this Pomeranian puppy—small dogs make great pets and have a lot of love to give.

dogs. Your dog will not understand most of what you are saying, but will enjoy hearing the sound of your voice. Like most dogs, yours will be happy just to be near you.

Keeping a small dog as a pet means that you will have to take on new responsibilities. But owning a dog also has its great rewards. Give your small dog time, attention, training, and affection, and you will find that you have a loving and faithful friend.

Glossary

breeder—Someone who raises dogs of a certain breed.

breeds—Different types of dogs that share similar characteristics.

characteristics—Qualities or features.

coat—In dogs, it is the fur or hair on its body. For example, dogs can have long coats, short coats, or curly coats.

crate—A cage or kennel for a dog.

emperor—A ruler of a place, like a king or a queen.

fossil—Bones or other hardened remains of animals or plants that lived many thousands or millions of years ago.

housebroken—A dog that has been trained to go to the bathroom in a specific area, usually outdoors.

mixed-breed dog—Dogs that belong to two or more different breeds.

purebred dog—A dog that belongs to a certain kind of breed.

socialization—The process of getting a dog accustomed to being with people and other animals.

trait—A quality or feature.

veterinarian—A doctor who treats ill and injured animals.

Find Out More

Books

Barnes, Julia. *Pet Dogs*. Milwaukee, WI: Gareth Stevens, 2007.

Calmenson, Stephanie, and Jan Omerod. *May I Pet Your Dog? The How-To Guide for Kids Meeting Dogs (And Dogs Meeting Kids)*. New York: Clarion Books, 2007.

Coile, Caroline D. *The Dog Breed Bible*. Hauppauge, NY: Barron's Educational Series, 2007.

Crisp, Marty. *Everything Dog: What Kids Really Want to Know about Dogs*. Chanhassen, MN: Northwood Press, 2003.

Rayner, Matthew. *Dog*. Milwaukee, WI: Gareth Stevens, 2004.

Web Sites

American Kennel Club

http://www.akc.org/kids_juniors/index.cfm?nav_area=kids_juniors
The American Kennel Club's Web site for kids includes contests and activities, and a newsletter with articles on how to care for your dog. The site also has a list of different small dog breeds.

How to Love Your Dog: A Kid's Guide to Dog Care

http://loveyourdog.com/
This Web site contains a lot of information about caring for your dog.

Dog Play

http://www.dogplay.com/GettingDog/puppy.html
This Web site tells you all the things you need to know about being a good owner before you bring a puppy home.

About the Author

Joyce Hart is a freelance writer. Throughout her life, she has had many different types of dogs—big and small. All of her dogs have been mixed breeds. Ms. Hart had a small terrier-Pomeranian mix named Barkley. Barkley had long black and brown hair, and loved to bark. He also loved to hide in an open space under the house and then jump out whenever Ms. Hart walked by.

Index